MEMORIES FROM MY CHILDHOOD

By

Mary Grace Barefoot Estes

Memories From
My Childhood

By

Mary Grace Barefoot Estes

Transcribed by

Barbara L. Gingerich Rivas
July 2017
Norman, Oklahoma

Christmas Memories

My first recollection of Christmas, my sister, Lois, and I were little more than babies, and we were on the front porch because it was a rather warm day for Christmas season. We were undressing our big cuddly dolls Mother had made over from the year before. They were like new and actually new to us because Santa had brought them to us. Our Grandfather Barefoot came along, I can see him now with his long beard, and said: "Now girls, your mother sat up night after night dressing your dolls and there you go tearing them up!" I am sure Mother had another hard job trying to help us live that incident down with Grandfather.

Children were happy in those days with what they received for Christmas. Girls usually got books and a doll. I remember the first book I ever received other than a school book. It was called "Mable's Mishaps", a story about a little girl and how she overcame difficulty. There were always stockings stuffed with candy and oranges and maybe an apple. Mother would pop corn and make popcorn balls. Our brothers would get a toy, not always a big one, but a good sturdy toy of some sort. One time Homer got a little music box that played one tune only. I can sing it to this day! Once in later years I reminded Homer of his little music box and even hummed the tune for him and it didn't please him too well, or he pretended to be displeased. I don't blame him because he was a little too old for teasing.

My First Boy Friend

When I was twelve years of age I claimed a boy who was 13. He was such a fine boy and I would see him at church and at singings on Sunday evenings. We seldom spoke to each other just sat or stood and grinned at one another. It was at a Christmas Tree program that he gave me a small vanity case. When he saw I had gotten it from the tree he came over and offered to open it for me.

My family soon moved away and I never saw him again. He died a few years later I heard. Dick Smith was his name, and that took care of that. I believe it was appendicitis that caused his death.

I Remember Prairie Fires

I must have been five years old and I would go out to where my Papa was picking cotton and pick big balls of cotton and put them in Papa's sack. I got tired of that after a while and decided I rated a cotton sack of my own. Mother sewed two flour sacks together and made me a small sack about my size. I would soon get it full and drag it to Papa to shake down and stuff for me. When it was full it looked like a sack of sausage. I felt like I was a very important person and Papa took such an interest in me trying to be helpful. But one day I saw a big spider or a praying mantis and I certainly gave it wide berth!

One night after supper all the men in the neighborhood were alerted that a prairie fire had been started and the men knew what that meant. They all gathered water barrels, old sacks and blankets to take with them to fight the fire. The women and children stayed at home and watched and prayed that the fire would not spread to our cotton fields. Mother noticed me all crumpled up and sobbing out these words: "I am afraid it will burn my little cotton sack." I remember the incident so well. I was teased about my cotton sack for years as well as my fear of losing it.

I Remember New Words

I remember one day when I was about seven years old we had company for dinner. They were our neighbors and Mother served chicken and dumplings with new potatoes and other garden vegetables. The dish of chicken and dumplings was passed the second time to our neighbor, Eva Meggs, who was pretty large. She said: "I don't know if I should eat this or not, sometimes it goes against me," and her husband who was rather witty said; "Oh Eva, it's not the quality that goes against you it's the quantity." After they were gone I heard Mother and Papa talking and laughing about it and I insisted on knowing the meaning of the words, quantity and quality. I never forgot where I first heard them used nor have I forgotten their meaning.

I Remember Revival Meetings

When we were children we always got excited about going to the Big Meeting. Papa would finish the chores as early as possible so we could drive into Hickory, Indian Territory, to attend the revival under a brush arbor. The horses were hitched to the wagon and quilts spread for us to sit and sleep on when we came home after church, and away we would go. Always when we came in sight of the oil lamps under the arbor we could hardly wait to get out of the wagon. We managed to stay awake during the singing and testimonies, then we children would fall asleep on pallets at the edge of the arbor floor. When we grew older we sat up and listened to the preaching of the second coming of Christ and the Judgement Day. I would think and pray about it for days later in my childish way and hope it would not come before I grew up and could have my own home and family.

I Remember School Days

I remember the death of a little girl at Hickory. She was a friend of mine. There was a plum tree in the school yard and it was a temptation to us to eat the plums not yet even ripe. This little girl ate too many and it made her sick and she died. Her name was May Milburn. It was such a sad day for all the children at school. We used to play house under the trees near the school at recess. We would sweep off a spot with a weed broom, and pick up broken glass and dishes for our china. We would turn a bucket upside down for a table and be at home.

I have played many an hour in such a play house all by myself. All my life I thought of the time when I could keep house and be a good wife and mother. That was my highest ambition.

I Remember How We Kept Food

It seemed that only people who lived in towns and had a good job could afford screens for their doors. We had no screens on our country home doors, at least not until I was almost grown. We had no ice, because there was no way to keep it. It was difficult to keep food from spoiling from meal to meal. We most always cooked three fresh meals each day. We would wrap wet clothes around the bowls of butter, and set them with pails of milk into a big bucket and lower it all to float on the water in the well. Sometimes we would set them in the creek and they would be as cold and good when we took them out at meal time.

I did not have an ice box until I married and ice could be bought and delivered. We usually bought 50 pounds at a time. But when I was at home there was no ice delivered! We covered all foods to keep insects out and at meal time we waved three branches over the table to keep bugs and flies away from the table.

I Remember a Trip

I remember my parents taking time to take us all to Sulphur Springs, Oklahoma, Indian Territory then, to an all day picnic and Old Soldiers Reunion. Papa put the cover over the wagon and we children and Grandmother sat in the back on quilts or spring seats. There was a big box of good smelling food all packed and waiting for the right time for us to eat. Sometimes I think this was the most important thing about the trip, just waiting for time to eat! We have always had so much fun at meal time. Well, when we finally arrived at Sulphur Springs there were beautiful parks for everyone to enjoy. The horses were taken care of and we began to enjoy the noise and bustle of people crying their wares for sale such as: "right over this away to get your taffy", or "here is your lemon-ade made in the shade, stirred with a spade, good enough for any old maid." Pink lemonade was new I guess, anyway everybody had to have that. It was made in a bright No. 3 wash tub with dippers hanging all around the rim and all you could drink for a nickel!

I remember Papa was a Mason. He belonged to the lodge the last nine years of his life. In all that time our Mother said, he never missed a monthly meeting. He rode his horse about three miles to Hickory lodge. I remember men who came to our house at night for Papa to give them the Secret work called "Lecture". It was all memorized and was not to be written down. I remember Papa lighting the coal oil lantern and going to the dugout to give those lectures. We thought that

so strange, and then our Mother joined the Eastern Star. She was Worthy Matron after Papa died. My Grandfather Barefoot and Uncle John were both Masons.

To Texas in a Wagon

My parents were from Texas. Papa, a native of Bell Co. and Mother was born in Tennessee but had lived in Texas most of her life. We moved to Indian Territory in 1894. I was two years old at that time and when I was five, my sister Lois was seven and Homer was four, and I believe Demp was two. Mother was so homesick for her kinspeople in Texas, she was little more than a girl herself that Papa decided we'd go to Texas when the crops were laid by. I can see that covered wagon and the horses hitched to it now! Dolly was the name of one of the horses. I think her colt had to follow as he was not weaned. It was a great trip in a way, especially for us children when we stopped to eat, no not at a café. We opened the grub box and enjoyed the good things Mother had prepared right in the wagon or in the shade of a tree. It took about a week to make the trip. We had to buy some food along the way I am sure. We slept in the wagon yards when night came or camped out. I can't remember the particulars, but I know we did spend one night going or coming in Dallas with friends by the name of Smith. By the way, they were the parents of the woman that I mentioned eating the dumplings.

Mother didn't get much out of the trip because Homer was playing with a stick which was used for discipline purposes and accidentally struck Grandmother Polly's eye. Well, that gave her a lot of pain and the result was that she lost that eye later. Then Homer had a big boil to come on his seat so in a way it was a miserable trip. It took us a week to get to Hillsboro, Texas from 15 miles East of Davis, Oklahoma. One can make the trip today in a day or even half a day. But covered wagon was all we had then. We spent one hectic week (for our parents at least) in Texas then the long trek back home. Our poor mother said, "I am satisfied to stay put, never again." And she never made that trip again for thirty years and then by automobile.

I Remember Cold Weather

Cold winter days were common then. We were small children and glad when it was too bad to walk the two miles to school. But, woe unto dear Grandmother and our Mother: 11 people housed up in a small house all day with restless children. Grandmother taught us guessing games she made up like this: "I know a man and wife and so many kids, 3 or 4, so many girls and so many boys." We all had to guess 'til we found the right answer as to whose family it was. We made Authors out of cardboard. We loved that 'till someone would get mad and out of sorts then the cards were taken away for the day' 'till we could be peaceable again. Then in the evening Mother would pop a big pan of corn and we'd have a party. I remember how Papa enjoyed popcorn. He would make a little funnel out of

newspaper and fill it then lean his head back and funnel
the corn into his mouth. He was not much more than
a boy at that time. I remember how sincere he was in
his Christian life. I have seen him retrieve a piece of
bread one of us had thrown in the ash bucket. He'd
say" "Never burn bread, give it to a chicken, dog or
birds, but never burn bread." Bread was sacred food to
him. I learned a great lesson right there.

I Remember Uncle Duncan

I remember when my Uncle Duncan (called Dunk)
married the second time after living a widower many
years. He married a lady (and she was truly a lady in
every sense of the word) from Kansas City. He met her
somewhere while visiting in Texas where she worked
as a nurse. He brought her home to live across the yard
from us. Afterwards her little daughter about nine
years old came from Kansas City to live with them and
to be our cousin. Oh, how proud we were to have such
a lovely playmate. She was a lovely child with big
sparkling blue eyes and long golden hair in braids and
curly bangs. Her name was Amy Conyers. Her ways
were different. She talked so softly and laughed such a
happy rippling laugh. We accepted her and
surprisingly this little city bred child accepted us. All
was new to her. The tiny house out back (out-door
toilet) was all fun to her. We initiated her into a lot of
things like crawdad fishing, dogwood tooth brushes,
picking wild violets down on the creek hunting ducks
nests, climbing haystacks and playing in cotton seed

bins, 'til Papa put a stop to that. He said we messed it up so the cows wouldn't eat it! But oh, how we loved Amy. She grew up in our family. Her mother died early. She and my Uncle Dunk had three children, Floyd, Hazel and Jessie. Floyd made a wonderful man and died years later. Jessie is now Mrs. Jessie Thomas living near Oklahoma City. Hazel lives in California and Amy married Charles Buckley and moved to Austin, Texas. Her husband was a photographer and was in business for years. He died in 1967 and Amy has continued to make her home in Austin alone. They never had children. I visit her when I go to see Gertrude and Loyce. She always seems content and always smiling.

I Remember When I Was a Little Girl

I remember when I was a little girl. Papa and Uncle John owned hay bailers and a wheat binder. These two men were very close for brothers and seemingly the best of friends. Uncle John was five or six years older than Papa, but they worked together and were laborers together in so many things. They cut and bound wheat for themselves and for others. I remember one man who was afraid he would lose his wheat if it stood any longer. So he persuaded the Barefoot brothers to cut his wheat on Sunday. Papa said they had trouble with the binder all day and that "never again will I work like that on Sunday!" I am sure Uncle John felt the same way.

I loved to go turkey nest hunting with Aunt Clara. She had twelve children but she would say, "Grace, an old turkey has hid her nest on the
creek some place, I'm sure she is setting so come with me and we will slip along behind her and keep out of sight and follow her to her nest." The old turkey came to the house for food and when she started toward the timber we trailed her and found her nest so we could watch for the hatching day.

At sorghum making time I remember seeing men going into the cane field with long knives to strip the fodder off, then someone came behind with a wagon to cut the cane and pile it on the wagon and take it to the mill. The juice would drip through cracks of the wagon bed on the way to the mill, where it was thrown into a large hopper and on it went until the juice was boiling. Men would skim the green foam from off the top and cook it until the juice became the right color and thickness. This took hours to do. Then they would pour the juice into big barrels. It took a lot of sorghum for our family and ten other Barefoot families. We sold some of it in the community and some we gave away. It took two horses to turn the mill as they were driven round and round by small boys. Believe me, boys and horses were ready to rest when night came.   When all the hired help came to eat they surrounded our big long table filled with hot biscuits, butter, sorghum, ham, potatoes and beans and all the good things a farm can produce. When the workers would leave after a meal we kids would clean up dishes and put things away and laugh when we counted 15 pickled peach seeds by one man's plate.

I Remember Butchering Time

I remember how men thought they needed a really cold day to kill hogs and they did then, with no refrigeration. When all the men came together for the preparations, I remember their breathing sent up spirals of steam like smoke. I can see the men working after the hogs were put to death. They would scald them in big wooden barrels, and oh, it looked awful, and yet it was thrilling. After this was done they scraped the hog and hung it on a scaffold or a tree, ripped open its stomach and cleaned and washed them down good and then took them down and cut them up. The women folk were waiting to finish
cutting up the special parts of the meat and to cook tenderloin and liver for the first big meal of fresh meat. One time a family was camping nearby and the man came and asked for the lights (which are the lungs of the hog), we never ate them. I am sure he was given some liver too. We all enjoyed the ribs, sausage and of course ham. The women would work for days grinding sausage and sacking it in large narrow sacks, and rendering the fat taken from the hog to make gallons of fine white lard. The cracklings were used for shortening bread and to make big pots of soap.

I Remember My First Balloon

My very first balloon was a hog's bladder washed and blown up like the little toy of today. Youngsters would fight over who would blow it up next, and it was lots of fun 'til it became good and dry then look out for the big blow up!

I Remember My Father's Death

I am really drawing the curtain back a lot. I have told what happened after my father's death. At least the sorghum mill story is. Papa died December 1901. It seems like hundreds of years ago. In such a different world. He was very ill for three weeks with pneumonia. It was such a dark time for us and our twenty eight year old mother with nothing of this world's goods but about 20 head of cattle and living on leased land. Our grandmother, Polly Harvey, lived with us. She was mother's foster Mother. My Mother, Sue Elizabeth Harvey had a twin sister
who only lived one year. My grandfather Harvey was a nephew of a Mr. Emery Harvey who was Polly Harvey's husband. Of course my grandfather, Tom Harvey, could not keep the little twins. Their mother died at their birth and her people took mother's twin sister. Uncle Emery Harvey and Polly (Aunt Polly to so many and really was my father's own aunt) took mother as her own child. Polly had just lost a baby of her own. She took mother and nursed her at the breast. She was my grandmother Barefoot's own sister, Polly Mobley was her maiden name. She was indeed Papa's own aunt. Our great Aunt Polly but, because Mother called her Ma the only mother she ever knew, we always said Grandma Polly. A dear old soul she was. Papa is buried at Hickory, Oklahoma, where a host of our people lie sleeping on the hill.

Pearl Barefoot Daugherty, my oldest cousin, was with us when Papa died. She had gathered us children together in the storm cellar to read to us. She read a funny story from the Dallas Semi (it was then) Weekly News. It was night and Pearl had lit the old oil lamp to read by. When Mr. Milburn, a neighbor, came and opened the door and asked, "Where are Joe's children?" we knew what had happened. Our Papa was gone, he who was so young with so much to live for, was gone from this earth. But, this is life and Pearl fulfilled her purpose by getting us out of the house.

Our mother was so young and broken-hearted, but she looked up to God, with a brave face and heavy heart she made out. She was determined to do so. She raised us and kept us all together. Our Uncle Harvey, Mother's young brother was visiting us from Tennessee when Papa died. Mother persuaded him to stay and put in the crop and he stayed 'til crops were almost laid by and because he was so homesick Mother let him go back home to his mother and sweetheart, Nellie, whom he married later. He helped us children so much though. That sad winter his youthful age, twenty or twenty one years, helped him to do so many wonderful things of humor for us.

He thought it an awful crime that we didn't have Grimm's Fairy Tales and so when he went home he sent it back to us. He told the funniest stories and sang silly songs for our amusement. From near Hickory we moved to Wynnewood, Oklahoma to a community called Carr Flat. This is the community where the sorghum making took place.

I remember becoming a teen ager. Uncle John's girls and boys, my sister, Lois, and I made up a large part of the young people of the community. Pearl had married. Vivian was grown. Pattie, four years younger than I would not read for herself and bugged me no end to give a whole book report on those I had read, such as <u>Lena Rivers</u>, <u>English Orphans</u>, <u>Dora Dean</u>, <u>Darkness and Daylight</u>, all by Mary J. Holmes.

We did a lot of horseback riding in those days, our only way to travel unless we went in the big wagon which we all did sometimes. We had lots of parties and lots of fun. We played such games as snap, fruit-basket turned over, slap in and slap out, all great party games of that day. The horse I rode most was named Susie. She was a little white pony. I thought I was really something when I dared to lope her as fast as she would go. Naturally, girls rode sidesaddle then.

More Memories from the Shadows

While living at Carr Flat Community the typhoid fever struck. Art Williams, a cousin living nearby took it first. Uncle John had him moved with his wife who was pregnant, to his house so they could help care for him. From that case Vivian, then 16, and Dick 14, both came down with it. Art got well but Vivian was ill a long time and Dick died. What a crushing experience for us all. I was in and out of the home trying to help. I carried water and ice to the sick ones though I was only 12. I helped Aunt Clara a lot. Mama didn't realize how contagious it was, no one did. After Dick died in a few

days I came down with it. I did not have a severe case. Had fever several weeks but the worst part about it you can't eat and eating was always half of my fun of living! I remember I had my chin covered with fever blisters for days after I got over the fever.

I remember Mother had to hire help on the farm. We raised cotton and corn. In the spring we helped make garden and planted flowers in the yard. Later we chopped cotton and helped thin corn and cut big weeds. My mother worked along with us while Grandma Polly kept the house and did the cooking, the dear old soul. My mother said she never could have made it without Grandma Polly. We walked about three miles to school in the most backwoods place you ever saw. But, a wonderful teacher with grades from one through eight, and all in one room. The years flew by and at last it found us no longer children but teenage youth, with a lot of work to do and some work we didn't care about doing. My sister and I pieced quilts and made beautiful embroidered things for our hope chests.

When we were in our early teens mother paid down on a place near Cement, Oklahoma. There was a nice house and several acres of land. It was to be our home and we planned to build more room as we could. School was only a block away. The boys and I attended this school. We drove a few miles to Sunday School and went to Sunday singings and preaching once a month. We had a neat little buggy, but, that horse was so lazy

the hired help would not even use him! We would have to use the buggy whip on him! Old Chub was his name and fat as a butterball, really a beautiful horse. Good to look at and that was all. We were very young ladies now in a new home and new surroundings. We were anxious to meet new people our age. I well remember the first time I met any of the new friends. We had seen one young man pass the house going toward the Country Store. His name was Jess Hutton and he wore a derby and I believe on that day he was using a cane (carrying it, you know) trying to impress the Barefoot sisters whom he had seen at a distance.

When I Met Sam Estes

I remember a young man we had met at Fair View came to visit us and suggested the three of us, he, Lois, and I, walk down to the Lutons. It was about 6 p.m. on Saturday and we had no idea who all we would meet at the Lutons but there I met some people, one especially who changed my life completely. I met Jesse Luton and Sam Estes and his family, his sister Eva was there, a young widow with three small children. A sing song was the program and what a good strong voice leading the singing! It was Father Estes and Eva was at the organ. Jesse Luton was a good tenor and Sam Estes a good low (timid) bass. Sam had on overalls. I don't remember any cake cutting or coffee drinking but as we were getting our coats to leave Jesse asked, "May I see you home?"

This was my very first date, I was just 14. I do not remember anything we said on the half mile walk except Jesse said, "Please excuse my garb." I thought "garb" a funny word. He had on clean striped overalls like farm boys wore. We went together pretty regularly for about five months and then Jesse left the County for other work and we both became interested in other people. We were just kids, and never were serious about each other. Had lots of good times though. He and his sister Mattie visited in our home a lot. Jesse played the Mandolin and sang cute songs of that day.

I remember seeing Sam Estes at the school house after that all dressed up always talking to other girls and never looking my way. He was only 18 but, I thought he must surely be 22 or 23 years old. I paid him very little mind only to think how handsome he was. He was keeping company with a girl who lived near us by the name of Volie Noakes. Once he dated my sister Lois, but, only once. He said they were too much alike about talking. The weeks and months went by after Jesse and I were not going together anymore. One Sunday evening there was a singing at Fair View and this tall handsome, reserved, older man Sam, caught me on my way out to our wagon to join my folks. To my surprise he asked to take me home in his new "hug-me-tight" red wheeled buggy. Driving a trim Sorrel horse with a star in the forehead! If I'd had false teeth I think I would have swallowed them. The idea was laughable that he, the silent type would be interested in a giggling high spirited girl like Grace Barefoot. Oh, did I ever say yes! You bet I did and quick!

I suppose you would think everything was smooth sailing and lovely between the two of us after that but you are mistaken. We didn't date each Sunday, just each two weeks. This tall Texan in Oklahoma wanted to be fair to all and give other fellows a chance. I think now it wasn't because he was so generous but because he had such a good opinion of himself! He thought he had it made! And he was right, he did, but, I hated him for his liberality and told him so. We knew that someday we would get married or at least we planned to.

My mother remarried while living in Cement. She married Tom Withrow, a man whom I had known all my life as he was Aunt Clara Barefoot's brother. The first time Mother married Uncle John Barefoot's brother, Joe, and the second time she married Uncle John's wife's brother. From this union Richard Dean and J. T. whom we loved as our own brothers were born. Tom, as we all called him, had attended music school and was taught by F. L. Eilland and Emmett S. Dean. For a man with little education he really knew old time system of teaching music. He understood music and was a good bass singer too. Well he taught several singing schools at night, ten night schools for $40.00 and $50.00. Lois and I went with him which was our chance to see Sam who was a music student. I didn't learn too much, I didn't try very hard. Sister played the old pump organ and learned a lot.

We moved to a place near Alex, Oklahoma and my heart was broken to move that far away from Sam because I had promised to marry him. We moved by wagons in one day. Our dear old grandmother died that first year and was buried at Alex. I think of that one grave to this day, and not another relative buried there and none living in miles of Alex. Sam managed to come to see me as often as he could. We broke up two or three times because we were too poor to marry and we'd argue about it. The last time we broke up my family was living at Criner, just a wide place in the road about 10 miles northeast of Lindsay, Oklahoma. I hadn't heard from Sam in two or three months. I was heart sick and disgusted having to live the way I was and so down-hearted, and thinking of getting a job somewhere when lo and behold a letter came in October from Sam wanting to come to see me.

He set a date for our marriage at Christmas! I can't remember when he came but we set our wedding date sitting at the kitchen table with an oil cloth on it, and a coal oil lamp. The date was April 18, 1911 and I had to do some shopping and my cousin Vivian Barefoot who lived near Blanchard had me to come there and she helped me pick out my small wardrobe and made my wedding dress, gown and slip.

Sam had to come to Chickasha and then to Purcell by train to get our license then he went to Lindsay and hired a rig to come on out to Criner and it was 10 or 12 miles. He said the guy that brought him out just fooled along! We were to be married at 3 p.m. and it was after 3:30 when he got there. I asked if he told the guy he was getting married and to hurry? No, he said, he was too timid to tell him. But it was a great day, so balmy and light showers and we walked about two blocks to the Methodist preacher's house. He read the ceremony in five or six minutes. His name was Rev. James Speedi. He was in a big hurry to go to conference. His wife and Mrs. Eva Young were our witnesses.

We spent that night at home and mother had chicken and cake for supper. I don't remember what else. Poor mother that was just two months before J.T. was born and how badly I hated to leave her. The next day we left for Lindsay and on to Chickasha by train. We spent the second night at Aunt Ollie's and then on out to the Estes farm the next day. I had all my earthly goods packed in one big pine box, except that few clothes I had brought in a trunk. The trunk made it by the time we did but it was several days before my box of things came. My feather bed, quilts, and pillows were in the box too. Uncle Tom, Sam's brother came out to welcome us into the family the first week. He was a big tease and grandfather and grandmother Standifer were there too.

We had an upstairs room for our own. It turned out that we stayed that first year from April 'till January with the Estes family. Sam had his crop in and it gave us time to find a house and helped us too. Of course, no farmer moves until the first of each year any way! So in January we got a neat little house and how happy we were to be to ourselves! It was good for me to live that first year with Sam's parents because I learned a lot about responsibility and hot to control myself, and to be considerate of others. We had very little to furnish a house with. I had 9 new quilts and sheets, pretty pillow cases all embroidered and trimmed. We bought a second hand round dining table and chairs and a 6 eye cook stove. We also found a dressing table and mirror and extra chairs. I made a big braid rug while living at his parents and Sam had a bed. Little did we think what our real life's work was to be. We were both people with open minds and hearts full of love for each other.

I remember how we were expecting a gang to come to give us a chivaree the night we moved in so we pulled down the window shades and blew out the lamps as though we were already in bed, but sure enough they came! They had horns, cow bells, and tin pans and what have you. We were ready for them with candy and cigars and invited them in for an hour of fun. Charles, Sam's oldest brother, came in a few days and brought his son John Dillen who was about four years old. They drove into town and brought back a beautiful set of dinner plates, our first ones. He said he asked John what he wanted to buy and John said "a broom" so John D. bought our first broom.

The first year to ourselves was filled with lots of work and planning for our baby. I will not go into that. Maybe someday I can take it from here and write, but there was a lot of heartache and a lot of joy and contentment in the many years we were together. I thank God for my Christian heritage, for my wonderful husband who said I helped him to become a Christian and I am thankful for his faith and his love and loyalty to me and to God and our children.

More Looking Back

I date my conversion to the Christian Faith at the age of 15 in a revival meeting with Rev. Buddy Robinson preaching. He was a Nazarene and a great preacher in his day. But I really think I was truly converted at the age of seven. I remember going to the mourners' bench at the Methodist Church at Hickory and just felt so condemned. I cried my heart out. I think Papa came and talked to me. I remember how I always prayed after that, but I was always afraid I would lose my religion. I was such a wicked little sinner that it took most of my time asking God to save me again until at last I just decided I was lost for good until about 15 years of age I really became better satisfied with my experience. I was about 18 before I ever joined the church, a Methodist Church. It was located at Blanchard and there was none nearer 'til we moved to Criner. I joined the church there before I married. There was a Methodist Protestant Church on Grand Dad Estes's place. He gave the land and I joined there

after I married. Sam was a Methodist too until we joined the Cumberland Presbyterian Church and Margaret joined with us at Little Rush Church near Rush Springs while Rev. Gene Bell was pastor. It was too far for us to attend regularly before Sam entered the ministry. We lived on what we call the Homer Bailey place and later moved to Wagoner and met Rev. O.N. Baucom and from there Sam started his life's work.

I think of many little incidents that might be interesting for someone, but I can't write it all now. When we were small children living near Hickory, a visitor, even a transient one, was exciting to us. One in particular was an old fellow by the name of Cum Polk. He was a peddler, and came around ever so often in a covered cart like a rig drawn by one horse. We always followed mother out to his wagon. He sold some cotton material and combs, lace and braid, and what have you. Sometimes he would accept eggs, butter etc. in exchange for what he had to sell. He always joked and laughed and this was interesting to us.

I told you about the times when sister and I were in our first school. Sometimes the snow would be so deep in the winter and it would be too cold for us to walk the two and one half miles so Papa would saddle old Jim, the big bay horse, and take me up in front of him in the saddle and sister would ride behind holding tight around his waist. Mother told us that Papa said if he lived his little girls were going to have an education, but of course he died before realizing that dream.

I remember Uncle John's children went to the same school and we usually had six at one time, or he did, in the school. Aunt Clara could not always prepare the lunch for their children before it was time for them to go. I remember several times when one of them would stay until she got the lunches all ready and then here he'd come about noon carrying a big bucket of food. Cousin Pearl, whom I mentioned before, was the oldest. She was in the 8th grade and an honor student, most a genius in math. She was a great comfort to me and to my sister. If I could look around and locate Pearl I was not homesick at school. I remember my teacher saying a very nice thing about me! I was a great reader, and I would get a new book given to me every few days. I was in the first grade and the old professor was lecturing the whole school one morning. He said, "If you were all as studious as this child here (pointing to me) we'd get along just fine." That was really a nice boost to my ego!

I remember quarreling with a little boy. He said, "I'll tell professor and you'll get a whipping." That was after school. The next morning I expected any minute to be called up and punished before the class. I could not study, I turned cold and sick at my stomach, and finally called Sister. She told the teacher I was sick, so she got permission to go with me to Aunt Laurie Grubbs' house. She was Papa's sister who lived a few blocks away. Aunt Laurie felt of my face to see if I had fever, and tucked me in bed and there I stayed from morning recess 'til time to go home, just sick with fear. I never heard a word about the affair anymore. I don't think I ever told anyone about this before now, what really caused my illness.

A Thought about Christmas

I remember this big tree at Church all trimmed up with strings of popcorn, red bunting and cranberries. Santa was there in all his glory too. One of my little classmates got nothing but a big red apple off the tree. She was so pretty and happy looking and asked me if she could see my doll, and I really wanted to give it to her. I remember she was dressed so nice. I don't know why she got nothing. Hall was still just a baby and when we got home he said: "Santa cause didn't bat his eyes." He could see through the mask!

When Hall was born Demp was a little over two years old and was somewhat upset over the new baby who had his place in bed. Papa was holding Demp one night and asked him: "Don't you like your little brother, isn't he good?" Demp said: "Yes him gude but don't like him. I want you to take him to woch (rock) creek and fro him in." Of course we all laughed, but I am sure it was a sad day for little Demp.

Homer was such a little man. He was always so alert and said and did many things that made him seem older that he was. When he was about four it was blowing and snowing like everything. Homer slipped out to where one of the hired men was chopping stove wood. He was singing "Sweet Summer's Gone Away, Sweet Summer's Gone Away." It was a little song Mother and Papa had learned at a singing school.

He never forgot anything. He was a sensitive little boy. He had a little pink dot on his nose for a long time when he was a little tad and some of the Kin teased him about turning to an Indian.

Demp saw sister and me coming home from school one day and ran to meet us and said to sister Lois, "Ois, I chalowed a ock." Meaning he had swallowed a rock. What we didn't do was not heard of to get that rock!

I remember a storm came up one evening and Papa and Mother got us all in the cellar. Papa was inside holding the chain to keep the door shut and it blew him clear out but he never let go of that chain and got back in ok. The hail broke out some of our windows and did some damage to the barn as I remember.

Children in these times are so blessed, but they do not realize it. In our day we had no radio nor television. There were no telephones, excepting in very few homes. There was no refrigeration, no push button appliances of any kind. Everything was done the hard way. Wash on a rub board, heat water in big kettles out in the yard. We used number three tubs! We had few books. The Bible, a few little story books, like <u>Gulliver's Travels</u>. I remember Papa bought us two lovely books, "Apples of Gold" and "Pictures of Silver", and then a story of the Bible. We loved those books.

One thing we cherished was a beautiful pump organ to be treaded with the foot. It was of beautiful maple wood, a lovely piece of furniture too. Sister learned to play and we all loved to sing. I remember Sister playing and Papa standing by singing "The Haven of Rest"!

Well, I keep thinking of more and more but I must hush. I had several girlhood chums I'd love to mention but it takes too long.

I am sure I have made mistakes in the epistle but to the best of my memory it is all true happenings.

May you all enjoy reading it.

Mary Grace Barefoot Estes

Mary Grace Barefoot was born the 13th of February 1892 in Bell County, Texas. She was the daughter of Joel Henry and Susan Elizabeth (Harvey) Barefoot. Joel Henry was the son of John Tipton Barefoot (1823-1897). Mary Grace married the Reverend Samuel Russel Estes on the 18th of April 1911 in Criner, Oklahoma. Samuel was born the 21st of July 1888 in Meridian, Texas. He passed away the 5th of October 1966 in Fort Worth, Texas. Mary Grace died the 20th of October 1985 in Borger, Texas.